# The Rise and Fall of Satan 'The Accuser'

Copyright © 2009 by Tony L Smith

Published by Tony L Smith
through Lulu Press Inc.

All rights reserved. No part of this book may be reproduced in whole or part in any form without the expressed written consent of the publisher.

ISBN/EAN 978-0-557-14593-5

Cover design by Robin Guiney

All scripture quotations in this book are from the King James Version of the Holy Bible unless otherwise noted

How did satan rebel against God?

When was iniquity found in his heart?

How did he try to make himself like the most high?

What was the main theme of his deception?

How did God address him?

When and how is satan cast out of heaven?

Does man have any thing to do with satan's rebellion against God?

Does the church have any thing to do with satan's defeat?

If a mechanic had little or no understanding about your car, would you allow him to work on it? If a beautician or barber had never had any schooling or training as to properly treat your skin or hair, would you allow them to work on you? The understanding these professionals have make them effective in what they do.

Understanding is an important tool given by Holy Spirit to which the Father God can manifest his will and purpose on earth. Understanding empowers the believer to act with confidence in what the Father has revealed to his heart.

These revelations are very precious to me. As with most spiritual topics, the more you write and pray, the more the Spirit reveals a thread of truth through the scriptures concerning the subject you are writing about.
   I, among others fill unworthy for such awesome revelations to come through. Which proves the scripture that says that God is not a respecter of persons. He just loves willing ones.

# Introduction

It has been my observation that most doctrines concerning satan (the devil) and his association with fallen mankind are incomplete and lack some important truths.

Existing doctrine make the rebellion of satan and the fall of man separate in their origin.

Most foundational teachings tell or at least imply that satan rebelled and was cast out of heaven before the creation of man.

While this teaching has not been overruled thus far, I feel it important and even necessary to bring some insight to the subject. My reasoning is in hope that it will bring more response to the heart of born-again believers to their role in the plans of God in the earth. We are called to be an overcoming people to God's Glory.

Would it add fuel to your desire to overcome satan if you knew we were not just a bi-product that he pulled in on his own rebellion, but that we were very much involved in his wickedness totally when it began?

Satan: comes from a base word meaning to attack or accuse.

## Chapters

One.      The first accusation

Two.      Why didn't satan attack God straight out as an Angel?

Three.    Satan appearing before God

Four.     'Son of Man'

Five.     The replacement of the ruler

Six       Satan 'the accuser' has no power over innocence

Seven     Satan trying tp steal the 'right of innocence'

Eight     Roots of murder

Nine      The accuser, the Law, and mans rule

Ten       Innocence prevailed over 'the accuser'

Eleven    Now remains faith

Twelve    Guilt and iniquities

Thirteen  The prophets address satan and man amongst the Kings

Chapter one
# 'The First Accusation'
## Caused the separation of man and God

*Have you ever had someone cut in on a relationship that you had with a friend and start talking smack about that friend to you? Suppose they were so convincing that you believed them and you turned a narrow judgmental eye toward your friend. This is exactly what happened to the woman in the garden, she entered into a judgment view against God.*

Let us go back to the Garden when satan first tempted the race of <u>man</u>kind. There is a lot to be said about why he came to the wo<u>man</u>, but for now let us look at how he used <u>man</u>kind to make his attack on the throne of God in the first place.

Gen 3:1  Now the serpent was more subtil than any beast of the field which the LORD God had made. And he said unto the woman, Yea, hath God said, Ye shall not eat of every tree of the garden?

Gen 3:2  And the woman said unto the serpent, We may eat of the fruit of the trees of the garden:

Gen 3:3  But of the fruit of the tree which *is* in the midst of the garden, God hath said, Ye shall not eat of it, neither shall ye touch it, lest ye die.

Gen 3:4  And the serpent said unto the woman, Ye shall not surely die:

*Gen 3:5 For God doth know that in the day ye eat thereof, then your eyes shall be opened, and ye shall be as gods, knowing good and evil.*

In the Garden was the tree of the 'knowledge of good and evil.' You can be as gods (Eloheem) is what satan told her, knowing good and evil.

'You can decide for yourself what is good or bad'

'You can rule your own life',

'Make your own decisions' ,

'Be your own boss',

'Control your own life',

'Captain your own ship '

'You, yourself can decide right from wrong' .

Need I say more about what he was telling her! it's the same thing he tells us. He was trying to remove her from depending on God's voice and presence. 'You can know good and evil'. The serpent was saying they could live on their own, not having to trust God for their well being.

A good friend of mine says that he implied to her that God was holding something back from them. The serpent <u>accused</u> God of being unfair, and caused her to long for intimacy with good and evil.

This accusation that God was holding something back from them was the serpent's lie. The fact that the 'tree of the knowledge of good and evil' was truly in the garden proved that our loving Father was not holding anything back from them. Father God gave them the choice to love him. He didn't want lovers that could not fail, like preprogrammed robots. He wanted mankind to love him by their choice.

She made the decision to eat of that tree on her own, separate from the trust in their relationship with God.

Since all life comes from God, to decide apart from Him brings guilt and shame, which are pre-manifestations of death.

God was trying to make a covenant of trust with man by relationship, but man had chosen to make covenant with an accuser. This action polluted man's whole being with shadows of death.

## Chapter two
# 'Why didn't satan attack God straight out as an Angel?'
### Why was mankind employed in his rebellion?

*My wife and I have watched several movies lately. I have noticed in the good verses evil type action films that the bad guys are always threatening to harm the good guys wife or girlfriend, children and close family to control him. Even when evil cannot find access to hurt the hero character himself, it attaches itself to the closest ones to him, his family: in order to cause him pain and turmoil.*

It is important to understand the method and the effect of satans rebellion against God. This is probably the reason he waited till man was created, because his sphere of control would be greater.

These next statements are not meant in any way to belittle or make light of the nature of Angels, or their importance in the service of God. Angels are very important and are mighty servants. I hope to work hand in hand with them more as I understand the plans of God in *the earth.*

How many of you have had pets? Your heart can really grow to love and enjoy them. But at the same time they will never fill the same space reserved in your heart for your spouse, your children or even a best friend.

Why? Because they were not created in the same image and likeness that you were. Your relationship with your pet can never be as full as your relationship with your spouse, children, and friends. A pet can not fully understand your desires, thoughts or feelings, much less communicate them back to you.

If you have two drinking glasses the exact same size, one filled with a beverage and the other empty. You would be able to pour all of the beverage from one glass to the other because they are of the same image and likeness.

When God made Mankind, he made us in his own image and likeness because he wanted to interact and have fullness of fellowship with us. The creation of man was the only creation that this was said about.

I am not talking about our physical makeup, but our inner man. We were created to be a dwelling for the Lord God himself, not in part, but in fullness.

Gen 1:26 And God said, Let us make man in our image, after our likeness: and let them have dominion over the fish of the sea, and over the fowl of the air, and over the cattle, and over all the earth, and over every creeping thing that creepeth upon the earth.
Gen 1:27 So God created man in his own image, in the image of God created he him; male and female created he them.

He made us to be filled with Himself.

Gen 2:7 And the LORD God formed man of the dust of the ground, and breathed into his nostrils the breath of life; and man became a living soul.

We alone of all his creations can understand his heart and respond to his desires in a way no other of his creation can, even the angels. We were made with the capacity to embody the Lord God in his fullness. Even of Jesus it was said that the fullness of the Godhead bodily dwelled in him. God's entire will and desire embedded in a mans body as He intended it to be in the beginning, and still does today.

Col 2:8 Beware lest any man spoil you through philosophy and vain deceit, after the tradition of men, after the rudiments of the world, and not after Christ.
Col 2:9 For in him dwelleth all the fulness of the Godhead bodily.

So if satan wanted to exalt himself and attack

God; in which he can't, he attacks Mankind to hurt God. Maybe he was jealous of us, I don't know.

In one deceitful lie satan exalted himself by prompting mankind to do the same, by accusing God of being unjust. He was able to embody his lying accusations in a creation made in the image and likeness of God. He told mankind to be their own God, and that they didn't need to depend totally on God.

This is the reason for the double prophesies by Ezekiel and also Isaiah saying both (satan and man) were exalting themselves as god, then declaring both to be abased and brought down. These prophesies are talked about later in chapter 13. God promised to deal with satan and mankind at the same time, but only offering repentance to man.

## Chapter three
# 'Satan appearing before God'

*Nobody likes a tattletale.. There are.. times when it is necessary to bring something someone is doing to the proper attention for the safety of that person or the safety of the ones they may be treating wrong. In this case one would say this was a just and correct cause.*

*On the other hand the motive of a tattletale is to bring an unfavorable focus on the person being accused, to make them look bad, and to cause their guiltiness to be brought before a judge. In this case it is to destroy any favor that person might have in the judges eyes.*

*A tattletale will bring up the most meager flaws in our character, actions, decisions, and desires before our judge and Father God. All these things our Father already knows about us and seeks to heal them in us.*

*As he did in the book of Job, satan tries to prove that given a chance he will cause us to stumble.*

Job 1:6 Now there was a day when the sons of God came to present themselves <u>before</u> <u>the LORD</u>, and Satan came also among them.
Job 1:7 And the LORD said unto Satan, Whence comest thou? Then Satan answered the LORD, and said, From going to and fro in the earth, and from walking up and down in it.

Job 1:8  And the LORD said unto Satan, Hast thou considered my servant Job, that *there is* none like him in the earth, a perfect and an upright man, one that feareth God, and escheweth evil?
Job 1:9  Then Satan answered the LORD, and said, Doth Job fear God for nought?
Job 1:10  Hast not thou made an hedge about him, and about his house, and about all that he hath on every side? thou hast blessed the work of his hands, and his substance is increased in the land.
Job 1:11  But put forth thine hand now, and touch all that he hath, and he will curse thee to thy face.
Job 1:12  And the LORD said unto Satan, Behold, all that he hath is in thy power; only upon himself put not forth thine hand. So Satan went forth from the <u>presence of the LORD.</u>

*Job 2:1  Again there was a day when the sons of God came to present themselves before the LORD, and Satan came also among them to <u>present himself before the LORD.</u>*

## 'What's he doing up there'

It appears that satan is not only appearing in the presence God but that he actually has a right or position to accuse man before God.

Notice God didn't call for Michael at this time to come get satan out of his face but merely asked satan to consider the righteousness of Job, a Christ like man. It seems God knew satan was there to separate man from the heart of God. God turned the focus of satan on the good character of Job.

Today God has a tried foundation of good

character in a son of man that has been placed on earth.

Satan was accusing mankind before the presence of the Lord. How can an angelic being appear before the presence of God and accuse man if it was previously cast out of heaven?

We have been taught of three heavens, so the body of Christ mostly agrees that satan and other demonic forces can and do occupy the second heaven. I am not trying to argue about the third heaven, but I wanted you to see where satan has been going before the presence of God and bringing accusation against you and me, and truly the whole race of man.

To me it seems as if satan has some kind of right to be in Gods face. Maybe because man has been so guilty?

Even now before the throne, satan can accuse the creation that was made in God's image. This creation of man that the Father so loves is being held guilty before him.

How annoying it must be to have someone continually accuse the ones you love. These accusations must sting the Fathers heart, especially knowing satan is making correct accusations against his creation. By correct accusations I mean he is always bringing up to the Father our mistakes, shortcomings and failures.

So the Father through Jesus has made provision to forever have the accuser removed from before his face, and has also given his born-again sons power to remove satan from before their faces.

The following Chapters will bring more clarity to how the Father did this.

---------------------------

Now satan has successfully accused God to his Creation, and has accused man before his Creator.

Both acts of rebellion he still commits today, and causes us to continually do both, accuse God and accuse each other before God. This causes both the heavens and the earth to be literally polluted with accusations.

# Chapter four
# 'Son of Man'

*Owners play a different role than presidents do in a company. The owner has complete control and title to a business, yet he entrust it totally to his president. The owner does not come and change things himself, he calls for the president and shares his desires and will for the company. Then the owner issues the command for change. The owner allows the president to implement those desires and commands.*
*Mankind is Gods' president on earth.*


## What's so important about the 'son of man'?

Joh 5:26  For as the Father hath life in himself; so hath he given to the Son to have life in himself;
Joh 5:27  And hath given him authority to execute judgment also, because he is the <u>Son of man</u>.

The phrase 'son of man' appears in the New Testament at least eighty five times. At least eighty four of those times it refers to the life of Jesus in a human body. Thirty one of those eighty five times it refers to Jesus after his resurrected body came out of the tomb.
Although Jesus never denied being the son of

God, he seemed to make continual reference to himself before and after the resurrection as the 'son of man'. Below are a few of those times

Mat 9:6  But that ye may know that the <u>Son of man</u> hath power on earth to forgive sins, (then saith he to the sick of the palsy,) Arise, take up thy bed, and go unto thine house.

Mat 26:63  But Jesus held his peace. And the high priest answered and said unto him, I adjure thee by the living God, that thou tell us whether thou be the Christ, the Son of God.
Mat 26:64  Jesus saith unto him, Thou hast said: nevertheless I say unto you, Hereafter shall ye see the <u>Son of man</u> sitting on the right hand of power, and coming in the clouds of heaven.

Act 7:55  But he (Stephen), being full of the Holy Ghost, looked up stedfastly into heaven, and saw the glory of God, and Jesus standing on the right hand of God,
Act 7:56  And said, Behold, I see the heavens opened, and the <u>Son of man</u> standing on the right hand of God.

Jesus the Son of God, because he was a son of man was given the right to perform or execute the judgment, or acts and decrees of God upon the earth. John 5:27

Gen 1:26  And God said, Let us make man in our image, after our likeness: and let them <u>have dominion</u> over the fish of the sea, and over the fowl of the air, and over the cattle, and over all the earth, and over every creeping thing that creepeth upon the earth.
Gen 1:27  So God created man in his own image, in the image of God created he him; male and female created he them.
Gen 1:28  And God blessed them, and God said unto them, Be

fruitful, and multiply, and replenish the earth, <u>and subdue it: and have dominion</u> over the fish of the sea, and over the fowl of the air, and over every living thing that moveth upon the earth.

    The rulership given to Adam over the earth was never lost. One of the reasons satan tempted Adam was to subvert Divine rulership and change it to his wicked rulership. He could not override mans rule, only manipulate it.
    This rulership of man which was given by God was never removed after the fall of man. It only became an ungodly rulership controlled by satan the accuser. Man still remains in his original position of dominion.
    We must understand that God never removes his word which he speaks. When he gave man dominion, he never withdrew it. Satan has operated and ruled through the rightful office that God gave to man, the word of God spoken to man.

    Do you think satan would have any rule on the earth through the animals, plants, waters etc.. if man was not present? Satan cannot rule through or use someone or something that was not given dominion by God in the first place.
    Mankind became satans' puppet.

    If satan operates through man, then the

verses below are not just about satan being prince of this world by himself, but really refers to the union made between man and satan.

Joh 12:31  Now is the judgment of this world: now shall the prince of this world be cast out.

Joh 14:30  Hereafter I will not talk much with you: for the prince of this world cometh, and hath nothing in me.

Eph 2:2  Wherein in time past ye walked according to the course of this world, according to the prince of the power of the air, the spirit that now worketh in the children of disobedience:

## Chapter five
# The replacement of the ruler

*When the company owner mentioned in chapter five sees that the president of his company has been influenced in a negative way, he decides that the president's loyalty to him has been compromised. Then the owner has no choice but to remove the president from his position and replace him with another.*

God had to anoint another *son of man*. He had to fire the president and hire another president to reverse the curse and remove the pollution caused by accusations which filled the whole creation of heaven and earth.

Ezr 9:6  And said, O my God, I am ashamed and blush to lift up my face to thee, my God: for our iniquities are increased over *our* head, and our trespass is grown up unto the heavens.

So through the virgin birth God had seeded his Son into the earth as a 'son of man'.

The seed of accusation had to come into the race of man by way of the wo<u>man</u> in the garden, because she had the womb of reproduction. So also did the innocent seed have to come back into the race of man by way of a wo<u>man</u>.

The seed coming through a woman is a sign that a seed needs a womb or incubator to come into manifestation. The woman was the womb of Adam. She was never named Eve (mother of all living) till after the fall in Gen. 3. Adam, the male, named her in faith responding to the word God had just spoken to the serpent. This of course was the promise of a redeemer.

Gen 3:15 And I will put enmity between thee and the woman, and between thy seed and her seed; it shall bruise thy head, and thou shalt bruise his heel.
Gen 3:20 And Adam called his wife's name Eve; because she was the mother of all living.

So now satan had to face Jesus, a man in the human race that was innocent. This left him powerless to accuse the life of Jesus in the heavens and before God. Jesus could do anything the Father asked him to do.

All satan's temptations to cause Jesus to doubt, accept accusations against God, or vary from his Fathers will failed. Jesus who learned obedience through what he suffered remained in divine authority on earth because he maintained pure relationship with his heavenly father. He remained innocent all his life. Satan the accuser had nothing in him. Satan's poison never penetrated his heart.

Joh 14:30  Hereafter I will not talk much with you: for the <u>prince of this world</u> cometh, and hath nothing in me.

    Bringing Jesus into the Human race, and Jesus maintaining an innocent position was part one of the Father's plan to replace the president of his company. Or to replace the present ruler on earth.
    This plan will unfold more as we go along.

## Chapter six
# Satan 'the accuser' has no power over innocence

*Below we see Jesus rejoicing and telling his disciples to do the same because their names were written in heaven, because of their association with Him. This gave them the authority to cast out devils in his name. Jesus said he saw satan fall from heaven like lightning, which was his response to what his disciples had just done.*

Luk 10:17  And the seventy returned again with joy, saying, Lord, even the devils are subject unto us through thy name.
Luk 10:18  And he said unto them, I beheld Satan as lightning fall from heaven.
Luk 10:19  Behold, I give unto you power to tread on serpents and scorpions, and over all the power of the enemy: and nothing shall by any means hurt you.
Luk 10:20  Notwithstanding in this rejoice not, that the spirits are subject unto you; but rather rejoice, because your names are written in heaven.
Luk 10:21  In that hour Jesus rejoiced in spirit, and said, I thank thee, O Father, Lord of heaven and earth, that thou hast hid these things from the wise and prudent, and hast revealed them unto babes: even so, Father; for so it seemed good in thy sight.

To take verse 18 out of context claiming that when he referred to *seeing satan fall from heaven like lightning* was before mans creation is only to make Jesus seem boastful in the past. Jesus would have been belittling what his followers had just done.

He is very much referring to what they had just did. He saw satan fall from heaven like lightning as they exercised casting out demons in his name.

So to heal the sick and cast out devils is the act of making satan, the accuser fall from heaven like lightning.

Even before the crucifixion of Jesus, which overcame death and the grave, his name carried a reputation in the heavens as the perfect sinless man. So the disciples had authority in the heavens only by Jesus' name because he alone could not be rightly accused in heaven. The sick were being healed and demons cast out by the innocence of Jesus' name. The disciples operated under His <u>right</u> to do these things.

What I am saying is that the reason Jesus operated in such authority to heal the sick and cast out devils is because as a man he could not be blamed for violating his Fathers will. Therefore; satan could not stand between Jesus and the will of God his Father. Satan's accusations against Jesus carried no weight in the heavens.

Association with Jesus and being under his care and authority caused his disciples' names to be innocent in the heavens also, like babes, along with His name.

It is like their names were being shadowed or influenced by His name.

Chapter seven
# Satan trying to steal the 'right of innocence'

*A thief always comes to steal something that another has to use it for their own self serving purposes. You can only steal what the other truly has possession of. Jesus had something satan wanted.*

Mat 21:33  Hear another parable: There was a certain householder, which planted a vineyard, and hedged it round about, and digged a winepress in it, and built a tower, and let it out to husbandmen, and went into a far country:
Mat 21:34  And when the time of the fruit drew near, he sent his servants to the husbandmen, that they might receive the fruits of it.
Mat 21:35  And the husbandmen took his servants, and beat one, and killed another, and stoned another.
Mat 21:36  Again, he sent other servants more than the first: and they did unto them likewise.
Mat 21:37  But last of all he sent unto them his son, saying, They will reverence my son.
Mat 21:38  But when the husbandmen saw the son, they said among themselves, This is the heir; come, let us kill him, and let us seize on his inheritance.
Mat 21:39  And they caught him, and cast him out of the vineyard, and slew him.

The husbandmen, or caretakers in this parable recognized the heir of the house, the son. The one who had the 'right of possession' before the owner of the house. They wanted what the son possessed.

In this story the husbandmen, or caretakers represent carnal man under the influence of satan. Satan made the husbandmen think that if they killed the heir then it would give them his rights or inheritance before the Father God.

Satan could not make Jesus fall into sin. So he moved man to kill Jesus. Satan did this to take the right position before the Father that Jesus had. The position of innocence, or righteousness (right standing).

The Divine rulership that man forfeited in the garden when he allowed satan to puppet his dominion, satan actually told man he could get it back if the heir, (the son) was killed.

Later we will see how satan tried to take the position of innocence using the Law God gave mankind to rule with.

It is kind of ironic that the very innocence before God that Jesus came to give us freely, mankind was trying to steal. This he was trying to do before the completion of the atonement, and apart from willful submission to Gods rulership.

These things can only be received through humble submission to the only deserving heir, Jesus, not separate from him.

## Chapter eight
## 'Roots of murder'

*Every thought has a father or seed giver..*
*Ever motive began with a thought..*
*Every action came from a motive...*

Below Jesus explains where the desire to kill him came from that the Pharisees operated in.

Please note that Jesus was truly loving them trying to reveal the root of their actions, so repentance could come to them.

Joh 8:40 But now ye seek to kill me, a man that hath told you the truth, which I have heard of God: this did not Abraham.
Joh 8:41 Ye do the deeds of your father. Then said they to him, We be not born of fornication; we have one Father, even God.
Joh 8:42 Jesus said unto them, If God were your Father, ye would love me: for I proceeded forth and came from God; neither came I of myself, but he sent me.
Joh 8:43 Why do ye not understand my speech? even because ye cannot hear my word.
Joh 8:44 Ye are of your father the devil, and the lusts of your father ye will do. He was a murderer from the beginning, and abode not in the truth, because there is no truth in him. When he speaketh a lie, he speaketh of his own: for he is a liar, and the father of it.

The Pharisees and the Jews with them were being told by Jesus that their father was the devil (or traducer :*traduce means* false accuser, devil, slanderer, to say very critical or disparaging things about somebody or something) because they sought to kill him.

So the accuser or traducer fathered their desire to kill him. These were the men who took pride in the fact that God had entrusted them to exercise rulership on earth with the Law of Moses.

In the beginning satan became the first father of a lie by <u>accusing</u> Father God of holding something back from Adam.

The Religious rulers were trying to use their position as the carriers of Gods Law to <u>accuse</u> an innocent man and have him killed, which could only be accomplished by lies. Satan fathered this lie!

Thus false accusation is the seed suggested to our hearts that father's all murder. The tongue is the main weapon for this wicked act.

So we might examine our own motives and ask ourselves "who's been our daddy?"

## Chapter nine
## The accuser, the law, and mans' rule

*The Law was given by God to Moses for the Hebrews to rule mankind by. The priest of Jesus day had authority from God in the use of the Law. This needs to be understood in order to comprehend the removal of satan's rule. Mankind ruled with the Law of Moses by Gods given authority.*

Paul says in Romans that the Law is Holy and good. There is no error in Gods Law. So the only error was in the practice and the use of the Law, especially when its use became influenced by the accuser, satan.

Rom 7:12 Wherefore the law *is* holy, and the commandment holy, and just, and good.

So satan accused God in the beginning, and still does in many various ways.

Also as he did in Job he still accuses man before God. To help fuel his accusations satan has used the Law of Moses to keep mankind condemned before God.

'Except when he made his accusation against Jesus he made a big mistake'

## 'more on the replacement of the ruler'

John 12:27 Now is my soul troubled; and what shall I say? Father, save me from this hour: but for this cause came I unto this hour.
John 12:28 Father, glorify thy name. Then came there a voice from heaven, *saying*, I have both glorified *it*, and will glorify *it* again.
John 12:29 The people therefore, that stood by, and heard *it*, said that it thundered: others said, An angel spake to him.
John 12:30 Jesus answered and said, This voice came not because of me, but for your sakes.
John 12:31 Now is the judgment of this world: now shall the <u>prince of this world be cast out</u>.

We mostly have agreed that verse 31 talks of satans removal, but this verse means also and maybe more so the removal of satans rule through mankind. Since man was given dominion of the earth (Gen 1:26).
So is the prince of this world satan or man, or maybe both in unholy union?

Consider this again;
The only rule on earth satan has enjoyed has been through mankind.
No fallen or sinful mankind = No satanic rule.
The rulership of the earth was given to man is Gen 1:28. So satan gained rulership through man, who has never lost the dominion of the earth. This is why the

first Adams' rulership had to be destroyed in order for the dominion to be given to another Man. A man who fulfilled the whole Law. A resurrected Man! A man who could never be rightly accused.

So when Jesus became sin and died he pulled the plug on satans rule through mankind by taking the first Adams' rule to the death with him. Jesus in Gods reality destroyed fallen, sinful, accused and accusing man. In the perfect sense Jesus destroyed mankind's rule in His own body and soul by death. The marriage between mankind and satan (the accuser) has ended.

## Chapter ten
# 'Innocence prevailed over the accuser'

*There are times when a man or woman is put in prison when they are innocent... If their case gets examined thoroughly, they are proven truly innocent. When this happens the wrongfully accused has to be released from prison declaring 'innocent of charges'.*

Rom 1:3  Concerning his Son Jesus Christ our Lord, which was made of the seed of David according to the flesh;
Rom 1:4  And declared *to be* the Son of God with power, according to the spirit of holiness, by the resurrection from the dead:

    Because Jesus was innocent, blameless, holy, upright, not having done anything deserving death, perfectly sinless, the grave of the convicted could not hold him and he arose on the third day as a new race of Adam, never to have touched the tree of the knowledge of good and evil, never to have accepted an accusation against his father.
    So it is as if the Father addressed satan after the death of Jesus asking him to reveal the reason in the Law that gave him the right to

have mankind (with the Law he gave them) judge and kill Jesus.

So because there was no account of sin in him, satan was speechless. He had to release this 'son of man' thus declaring him 'Son of God' or the one full of <u>Gods nature and character</u> because he was <u>innocent</u> of all charges.

Death, Hell and the Grave had no claim on him.

Satan had accused the wrong man. Real innocent blood had been wrongfully shed using God's Law.

The law of Moses had been completely misused in the case of Jesus.

At last, the accuser (satan) stood accused of injustice, having to forfeit his rights to rule through man any more. The priestly right to use Gods Law to rule with was removed from the first Adam. Jesus became the Last of the first Adams' race.

Then at resurrection he became the second or the new Adam and the <u>new</u> high priest.

Innocence had triumphed over <u>accusation</u>! Jesus, the anointed resurrected man, alone has the right to rule.

**Mat 26:64** Jesus saith unto him, Thou hast said: nevertheless I say unto you, Hereafter shall ye see the **Son of man** sitting on the right hand of power, and coming in the clouds of heaven.

'Summery of chapters one through eight'
We have proved or at least implied that satan assaulted God and his creation in the garden, using man as his puppet. Jesus overturned satan's rule by being wrongfully condemned by man, thus breaking the satanic influence in his own body.

If man was used to pollute the heavens with accusations, then man has to be the one to cleanse the heavens with the innocence of Jesus by cooperation with the Spirit of God.

Jesus alone was able to initiate this work. Thus the seal was broken to the Fathers heart for his creation once again. Never before did the Father have a totally righteous life on the earth in which to establish his Divine Rulership through. Jesus' rulership could not be overturned by accusations because he was sinless.

At last, the Father God has a foundation in which to build and execute his purpose in the earth. His overcoming Son of innocence. The Government shall be upon his shoulders.

Finally, God no longer has to respond toward mankind by mercy alone, he now has a platform of righteousness: *the innocence of His 'son of man'*

The new dominion's cornerstone has been

laid, The temple building has been started. The call for builders is going out. Come and meet the new ruler, be covered by his blood, and join the construction of His Heavenly Kingdom on earth.

Divine rulership is on the scene!

Repent, the Kingdom of heaven is at hand.
Or as I like to put it.. 'Change the way you think and operate, the Rulership of another is here!

## Chapter eleven
## 'Now remains Faith'

*So what Now? If these things be true, then why is their so much wickedness and rebellion still going on in the earth? Why are our struggles not answered already?

*You know it is possible to own something and still not be in possession of it. You can pay for a car and not have it at your house and not be driving it, although you own the title deed.*

In the work of Jesus, Father God has repossessed the race of mankind and handed it over to another Man, The resurrected Jesus and his Christ . Rev 11:15. The ambassadors of this possession are you and I (His body on earth). We, his born-again body, with repossession papers in hand are to act in faith to complete the purchase that Jesus made.

As pointed out in the below verse truth has to be mixed with faith.

Heb 4:2  For unto us was the gospel preached, as well as unto them: but the word preached did not profit them, not being mixed with faith in them that heard *it*.

The Father needs his anointed ones to see,

comprehend, declare, decree and act upon the finished work of Calvary. Since now we are seated in heavenly places with the anointed Jesus, then we must cleanse the heavens and the earth with the Word of Truth.

The first half of the below verse talks about bringing the rulership of heaven to earth by way of revelation keys.

The second half of this verse is in a different order, first on earth then heaven. The revelation keys of the Kingdom are to be used to bind and loose on earth so as to bind and loose in the heavens, making what you say and do impact and change the heavens. Sounds kind of like making satan fall from heaven like lightning, doesn't it?

Mat 16:19 And I will give unto thee the keys of the kingdom of heaven: and whatsoever thou shalt bind on earth shall be bound in heaven: and whatsoever thou shalt loose on earth shall be loosed in heaven.

We see the keys being given to man in order to cause change in the heavens, which have been polluted by the accuser. In other words, is the space between us and the father still filled with accusations that keep us from understanding the Fathers will toward us?

We must believe our sins are forgiven by forgiving others. Stop the accuser, remove him from his unrighteous reign in the heavens. Let Jesus submit your case in His name to remove your accuser from before Gods' Throne.

Chapter twelve
# Guilt and iniquities

Ezr 9:6 And said, O my God, I am ashamed and blush to lift up my face to thee, my God: for our iniquities are increased over *our* head, and our trespass is grown up unto the heavens.

*There is no doubt that he who sins feels guilt and shame. There is also no doubt that this one cannot come out of his sin if they never truly understand that their sin is forgiven and that their sin nature is changed to a right or new nature founded upon the innocence of Jesus.*

Ezekiel implies that satan must have massive wings that were used to cover something.

**Eze 28:14** Thou *art* the anointed cherub that <u>covereth</u>; and I have set thee *so*: thou wast upon the holy mountain of God; thou hast walked up and down in the midst of the stones of fire.
Eze 28:15 Thou *wast* perfect in thy ways from the day that thou was created, till iniquity was found in thee.
Eze 28:16 By the multitude of thy merchandise they have filled the midst of thee with violence, and thou hast sinned: therefore I will cast thee as profane out of the mountain of God: and I will destroy thee, O <u>covering</u> cherub, from the midst of the stones of fire.

I'm not sure what satan actually was created to cover, except that it was a God given ability.

But now when these same wings are spread over you they cause darkness, guilt, shame, hopelessness, confusion, discontent, anger and so on...They make you feel accused. They separate you from the light of God.

Because of the finished work of Calvary, Holy Spirit has been sent to empower, enlighten, and transform us to Sons of innocence by the blood of Jesus.

---

Mat 24:29  Immediately after the tribulation of those days shall the sun be darkened, and the moon shall not give her light, and the stars shall fall from heaven, and the powers of the heavens shall be shaken:
Mat 24:30  And then shall appear the sign of the Son of man in heaven: and then shall all the tribes of the earth mourn, and they shall see the Son of man coming in the clouds of heaven with power and great glory.

What would the heavens being shaken and the appearance of the 'Son of Man' in heaven have in common?
Notice that Jesus didn't say the Son of God here. This is because the innocence of a 'son of man' appearing in heaven is what shakes the heavens and causes the accusers to be thrown down.
Allow me to use a comic book hero to explain more

clearly. In Gotham City when the Batman symbol was shot up in the sky it was to bring fear to the villains and hope to the common man.

In a similar way the appearance of Jesus, a son of man, in heaven brings fear to the accusers and hope to the accused. Demonic strongholds literally screech in fear and are cast down over regions as Jesus is Glorified. The powers of the heavens are shaken and the stars fall from the sky.


Eph 3:9  And to make all *men* see what *is* the fellowship of the mystery, which from the beginning of the world hath been hid in God, who created all things by Jesus Christ:
Eph 3:10  To the intent that now unto the <u>principalities and powers in heavenly *places*</u> might be known by the church the manifold wisdom of God,
Eph 3:11  According to the eternal purpose which he purposed in Christ Jesus our Lord:
Eph 3:12  In whom we have boldness and access with confidence by the faith of him.

----------------------------------


Rev 12:5  And she brought forth a man child, who was to rule all nations with a rod of iron: and her child was caught up unto God, and *to* his throne.


War broke out in the heavens when Jesus was caught up unto Gods' throne.  Verse 10 says that satan (the accuser) was cast out of heaven, and that salvation, the Kingdom of our God, and the power of his Christ (his anointing or anointed ones) has come.

Rev 12:7  And there was war in heaven: Michael and his angels fought against the dragon; and the dragon fought and his angels,
Rev 12:8  And prevailed not; neither was their place found any more in heaven.
Rev 12:9  And the great dragon was cast out, that old serpent, called the Devil, and Satan, which deceiveth the whole world: he was cast out into the earth, and his angels were cast out with him.
Rev 12:10  And I heard a loud voice saying in heaven, Now is come salvation, and strength, and the kingdom of our God, and the power of his Christ: for the accuser of our brethren is cast down, which accused them before our God day and night.
Rev 12:11  And they overcame him by the blood of the Lamb, and by the word of their testimony; and they loved not their lives unto the death.
Rev 12:12  Therefore rejoice, *ye* heavens, and ye that dwell in them. Woe to the inhabiters of the earth and of the sea! for the devil is come down unto you, having great wrath, because he knoweth that he hath but a short time.

Let me ask you a question now. Do you ever feel like accusations are filling the space between you and God? Do you still feel unworthy to walk in the favor of God. If you do, then satan still fills your heaven. He has been defeated by Jesus, but you still feel accused before God.

You must overcome him by the blood of the lamb and the word of your testimony. Surrender your life, return to God with all your heart.

Rev 12:11 And they overcame him by the blood of the Lamb, and by the word of their testimony; and they loved not their lives unto the death.

Complete what Jesus started and remove satan from your heaven, remove him from the space between your heart and the Fathers' heart. Allow the finished work of Calvary to cleanse you of all shame, guilt, and the inability to be innocent before your God. Let God restore your <u>innocence</u>. Submit to the goodness of God and be raised out of death, guilt and shame.

Then prove you are forgiven by releasing others.

For without faith it is impossible to please God, for all who come unto him must believe he is and is a rewarder of those who seek him with all their heart. Faith empowers you to act (even with emotion) upon the truth.

Anchor your faith in the innocence of Jesus shed blood! Which cries "Mercy" and "Forgive them, they know not what they do."

## Chapter Thirteen
# 'The prophets address satan and man amongst the Kings'

Back to the book of beginnings. Genesis'

Gen 2:8  And the LORD God planted a garden eastward in Eden; and there he put the man whom he had formed.
Gen 2:9  And out of the ground made the LORD God to grow every tree that is pleasant to the sight, and good for food; the tree of life also in the midst of the garden, and the tree of knowledge of good and evil.
Gen 2:15  And the LORD God took the man, and put him into the garden of Eden to dress it and to keep it.

We see that God created the garden and put man in it to care for it. We also see that the tree of life was there and also the tree of knowledge of good and evil. Below we also see that satan first appeared in scripture in the garden as a serpent where he tempted the woman.

Gen 3:1  Now the serpent was more subtle than any beast of the field which the LORD God had made. And he said unto the woman, Yea, hath God said, Ye shall not eat of every tree of the garden?

## Man and satan addressed by Ezekiel

Eze 28:1  The word of the LORD came again unto me, saying,
Eze 28:2  Son of man, say unto the prince of Tyrus, Thus saith

the Lord GOD; Because thine heart is lifted up, and thou hast said, I am a God, I sit in the seat of God, in the midst of the seas; yet thou art a man, and not God, though thou set thine heart as the heart of God:

In these verses above Ezekiel was told to address the prince (the commander) of Tyrus, In verse 2 Ezekiel calls him a man.
Below we see Ezekiel in the same chapter address the king of Tyrus, never referring to him as a man, but in verse 14 and 16 as an anointed and a covering cherub. Most believe this to be in reference to the devil or satan, which I agree.

Eze 28:11  Moreover the word of the LORD came unto me, saying,
Eze 28:12  Son of man, take up a lamentation upon the king of Tyrus, and say unto him, Thus saith the Lord GOD; Thou sealest up the sum, full of wisdom, and perfect in beauty.
Eze 28:13  Thou hast been in Eden the garden of God; every precious stone *was* thy covering, the sardius, topaz, and the diamond, the beryl, the onyx, and the jasper, the sapphire, the emerald, and the carbuncle, and gold: the workmanship of thy tabrets and of thy pipes was prepared in thee in the day that thou wast created.
Eze 28:14  Thou *art* the anointed cherub that covereth; and I have set thee *so*: thou wast upon the holy mountain of God; thou hast walked up and down in the midst of the stones of fire.
Eze 28:15  Thou *wast* perfect in thy ways from the day that thou wast created, till iniquity was found in thee.
Eze 28:16  By the multitude of thy merchandise they have filled the midst of thee with violence, and thou hast sinned: therefore I will cast thee as profane out of the mountain of

God: and I will destroy thee, O covering cherub, from the midst of the stones of fire.

*Eze 28:17 Thine heart was lifted up because of thy beauty, thou hast corrupted thy wisdom by reason of thy brightness: I will cast thee to the ground, I will lay thee before kings, that they may behold thee.*

Eze 28:18 Thou hast defiled thy sanctuaries by the multitude of thine iniquities, by the iniquity of thy traffic; therefore will I bring forth a fire from the midst of thee, it shall devour thee, and I will bring thee to ashes upon the earth in the sight of all them that behold thee.

Eze 28:19 All they that know thee among the people shall be astonished at thee: thou shalt be a terror, and never *shalt* thou *be* any more.

We see also in verse 13 that satan was in Eden, the garden of God and in verse 14 that he walked up an down in the midst of the stones of fire on the mountain of God.

Could this be the same garden that Adam was set in to care for in Genesis? If so, then maybe the stones of fire refer to mankind, as the New Testament calls believers flames of fire, living stones, and Jesus even changed Simon's name to Peter (a small rock).

So in Ezekiel 28 we see man and satan being addressed in similar fashion. No doubt the prince of Tyrus and the king of Tyrus occupy the same space of history here and are also involved in the same prideful movement by acting like they are the most high. One addressed by Ezekiel as a man, and the other addressed by Ezekiel as an angel (or covering cherub)

Although I'm not a Hebrew scholar, I have been told that most Hebrew language was not in past or future tense, but in present tense. So the best rendition of verse 16 where King James version says I will cast you from the mountain of God should be as a declaration. 'I cast you out of the mountain of God', making the decree neither past or future tense but present tense 'I cast'. The decree was not only promise but as an active verb being declared by Ezekiel.

Below we see the Lord through Isaiah address the king of Babylon and Lucifer much the same way that Ezekiel did the king and prince of Tyrus in the previous verses. In these references Lucifer claimed he will be like the most high, verse 13 and 14. Isaiah refers to Lucifer as a man in verse 15 promising him to be brought down to hell. Again maybe this is Lucifer appearing in man (the Kings) as to puppet them.

Isa 14:4 That thou shalt take up this proverb against the king of Babylon, and say, How hath the oppressor ceased! the golden city ceased!
Isa 14:5 The LORD hath broken the staff of the wicked, *and* the scepter of the rulers.

Isa 14:6  He who smote the people in wrath with a continual stroke, he that ruled the nations in anger, is persecuted, *and* none hindereth.
Isa 14:7  The whole earth is at rest, *and* is quiet: they break forth into singing.
Isa 14:8  Yea, the fir trees rejoice at thee, *and* the cedars of Lebanon, *saying*, Since thou art laid down, no feller is come up against us.
Isa 14:9  Hell from beneath is moved for thee to meet *thee* at thy coming: it stirreth up the dead for thee, *even* all the chief ones of the earth; it hath raised up from their thrones all the kings of the nations.
Isa 14:10  All they shall speak and say unto thee, Art thou also become weak as we? art thou become like unto us?
Isa 14:11  Thy pomp is brought down to the grave, *and* the noise of thy viols: the worm is spread under thee, and the worms cover thee.
**Isa 14:12**  How art thou fallen from heaven, O Lucifer, son of the morning! *how* art thou cut down to the ground, which didst weaken the nations!
Isa 14:13  For thou hast said in thine heart, I will ascend into heaven, I will exalt my throne above the stars of God: I will sit also upon the mount of the congregation, in the sides of the north:
Isa 14:14  I will ascend above the heights of the clouds; I will be like the most High.
Isa 14:15  Yet thou shalt be brought down to hell, to the sides of the pit.
Isa 14:16  They that see thee shall narrowly look upon thee, *and* consider thee, *saying, Is* this the man that made the earth to tremble, that did shake kingdoms;
Isa 14:17  *That* made the world as a wilderness, and destroyed the cities thereof; *that* opened not the house of his prisoners?

Here again we have both man and satan being addressed in mostly the same way by two major prophets.

---

Consider this conclusion of this small book. The prince of darkness and his reign on earth, and man's kingdom of 'self' are one and the same thing.

One did not start without the other, and one will not end without the other ending.

The man Jesus is the corner stone and the cap stone of this work. We must fill in the rest of the structure.

*Be blessed with revelation knowledge
and an overcoming heart.*

To purchase more copies of this book, or to buy the book in a downloadable format, go to

http://stores.lulu.com/store.php?fAcctID=4312948

http://www.lulu.com/content/paperback-book/the-rise-and-fall-of-satan-the-accuser/7689087

Or e-mail  Jehubooks@yahoo.com

Made in the USA
Lexington, KY
03 May 2010